Waiting to be Wanted

A Stepmom's Guide to Loving Before Being Loved

Companion Workbook

Cheryl Shumake

Waiting to be Wanted – Companion Workbook

©2021 by Cheryl Shumake

Published by Stepmom Sanity and The Inspired Studio, LLC

All rights reserved. No part of this book may be reproduced, stored in a retrieval system, or transmitted in any form or by any means – electronic, mechanical, photocopy, recording, or otherwise – without written permission of the publisher, except for brief quotations in reviews.

Distribution of this editions of this workbook in any format via the internet or any other means without the publisher's written permission or by license agreement is a violation of copyright law and is subject to substantial fines and penalties. Thank you for supporting the author's rights by purchasing only authorized editions.

The persons and events portrayed in this book have been used with permission. To protect the privacy of these individuals, some names and identifying details have been changed.

All Scripture quotations, unless otherwise indicated, are taken from the Holy Bible, New International Version®, NIV®. Copyright ©1973, 1978, 1984, 2011 by Biblica, Inc.™ Used by permission of Zondervan. All rights reserved worldwide. www.zondervan.comThe "NIV" and "New International Version" are trademarks registered in the United States Patent and Trademark Office by Biblica, Inc.™

Scripture quotations marked ESV are from the ESV® Bible (The Holy Bible, English Standard Version®), copyright © 2001 by Crossway, a publishing ministry of Good News Publishers. Used by permission. All rights reserved.

Scripture quotations marked MSG are taken from The Message. Copyright Â© 1993, 1994, 1995, 1996, 2000, 2001, 2002. Used by permission of NavPress Publishing Group.

ISBN: 978-1-7364025-1-1

Printed in the United States

Soli Deo Gloria

For the glory of God, alone!

TABLE OF CONTENTS

WELCOME 7

DIGGIN' IN 9

A FUNNY THING HAPPENED ON THE WAY TO BEING LOVED 13

SECTION I: THE FAMISHED HEART
MALNOURISHED MOMS 21
A HEART IN HIDING 25
SHARK BAIT 33
HOPE DEFERRED 43
CAN I GET OFF NOW? 51
EXERCISE: THRIVER IN HIDING 59
EXERCISE: EMOTIONAL VOCABULARY 61
SCRIPTURE MEDITATION 63
NOTES 66

SECTION II: THE FOCUSED HEART
MEASURED MOMS 73
SPARKED 77
THE (HE)ART OF RENEGOTIATION 85
SACRED STRATEGIES 93
STURDY LOVE 99
EXERCISE: WRITE YOUR STEPMOM MISSION STATEMENT 107
SCRIPTURE MEDITATION 113
NOTES 116

SECTION III: THE FRUITFUL HEART
MARVELING MOMS   123
FIRST AND FOREMOST   127
MY FATHER'S EYES   139
SAFE SHEPHERDS   149
THIS HEART IS ON FIRE   155
EXERCISE: THE DEVOTED LIFE   163
SCRIPTURE MEDITATION   165
NOTES   168

CONCLUSION
THE WAIT IS OVER   173
LETTER FROM A BIO MOM   175

RECOMMENDED RESOURCES   177

ACKNOWLEDGEMENTS   179

Hey there Stepmom Sister,

I'm so happy you're here. Thank you for adding this companion workbook to your Waiting to be Wanted journey. It's my way of walking alongside you, helping you dig deeper for truth, go farther towards freedom, and hold tighter to faith in God on behalf of your family.

Although the complexities of our blended life can make it hard to believe at times, God's intentions towards us are good. It doesn't "feel" like His intentions are good when bio-mom is using the children to hurt your husband. Or when your husband's mom does not acknowledge your child; her non-biological grandchild. It doesn't "feel" like God's intentions are good while you sit alone in the crowd at your kitchen table; once again shut out of the laughter and connection of shared history. Nevertheless, God decided that your family dynamics are exactly what was needed to complete His good work in and fulfill His good plans for you.

No matter where you are, or how you may feel, know that you are not alone; The Stepmom Sanity™ team has prayed for you; we believe in you, and we are rooting for you. Above all, the Holy Spirit is the One guiding you. He is with you for every turn of the page, insight revealed, and question asked. He is there to locate you, challenge you, and help you. Make your heart fully accessible to what He might want to teach you, and how He might want to transform the way you relate to your bonus children.

One more thing. If, after reading Waiting to be Wanted, and using the workbook, you'd still like to speak with someone, do not hesitate to reach out. You can email us at info@stepmomsanity.com.

Keep stepmomming in grace,

Cheryl

DIGGIN' IN

I want to help you get the most out of your Waiting to be Wanted Companion Workbook. This workbook is meant to enhance and support your pilgrimage through Waiting to be Wanted: A Stepmom's Guide to Loving Before Being Loved.

Like the book, the workbook is divided into three sections: The Famished Heart, The Focused Heart, and The Fruitful Heart. Each chapter in the workbook correlates to a main chapter in the book. You will find questions based on the material covered in that chapter, space to record your responses, along with additional stories and questions to expand on what you're discovering.

Additional features of this workbook include:

Treasure Hunt
Each main chapter in the book ends with an opportunity for us to penetrate beyond the surface and touch on deeper meaning in the chapter. That segment is called "Treasure Hunt." It is repeated in the workbook with space for you to record your responses.

Scripture Meditation
Each section of Waiting to be Wanted ends with a list of scriptures. The Scripture Meditation pages in this workbook offer space so you can write out and answer questions for up to three of the scriptures the Holy Spirit is drawing to your attention.

Working on It
I added tools and exercises to this workbook to help some of the principles take shape as you receive and apply truth. Those are at the end of each section.

Notes
No matter how thorough I am, you will ask more questions, make observations unique to you and your family, and want to jot down additional scriptures. I have added a "notes" page at the end of each section for that purpose.

I'm so grateful to be on this journey with you. It really is an honor. I'm also excited for you. You are on the cusp of a grand adventure. The scarred hand of our precious Lord Jesus is outstretched. Dear friend, place your hand in His, take a deep breath, and dive in!

How we wait determines if the waiting is *troubled* or *peace-filled.*

A FUNNY THING HAPPENED ON THE WAY TO BEING LOVED

Have you ever noticed how autocratic following Christ is to your flesh? Seriously. I mean, do you ever get to react to the craziness in your family how you really want to without that twinge of conviction from the Holy Spirit?

We can certainly override conviction, and I have from time to time, but life is much easier when we follow God's leading; no matter how hard doing so may be on our pride and ego.

Our black lab, Sarah Patches, was part of our family for 15 years. Sarah was a big, beautiful, muscley bundle of cuddles. Her antics became the stuff of family legend. She once snuck a banana out of Kayla's backpack, peeled and ate the banana, then left an intact peel on the couch. Sarah was huge, zany, and smart. So smart, she flunked obedience school…twice. Not because she didn't understand the commands. She just didn't want to follow them. Every time we threatened her with sleeping in her cage, she suddenly remembered how to sit, stay, get off, lay down, and stop.

Like many headstrong creatures, Sarah had a bit of wanderlust. Quite a few neighbors knocked on our door, at odd hours, with a jubilant pup in tow, wagging her tail, and giving us a big goofy smile. We could not figure out how she kept getting out of our fenced backyard. One day, I spied Sarah nosing the latch on the gate. Just as she made her way through the open gate, I rushed out of the sunroom and grabbed her collar. We began putting a railroad spike in the latch so she could not move it. Since our utility meters were in the backyard, we made sure the meter readers knew to replace the spike when they left through the gate. One day we had a substitute meter reader who did not know about replacing the railroad spike. By that evening, Sarah was on the run. It took two weeks to find her; holed up in a home 5 miles away with, thankfully, very nice people.

Sarah did not like being confined to the backyard, but we knew the possible dangers that awaited her outside the safety of the fence. The backyard seemed oppressive to her wanderlust. Sarah wanted to do what she wanted to do regardless of the impact on us or the danger to herself. She kept pushing at the limits until an opportunity to break free presented itself. The problem is, but for

God's mercy, self-serving freedom usually ends badly.

Loving before being loved places restrictions on my instinct to protect myself from being hurt, defend myself against misjudgment, and react to the thoughtless actions of others. Jesus says be patient when my wandering heart wants to lash out. He instructs me to forgive the tenth insult of the day while I'm still feeling the sting of the first. I have to step outside the fence to do what I want. However, acting without regard to the impact on people around me, or the danger to my soul within me, is costly. Is freedom really freedom if it leads to bondage?

When waiting to be wanted, we are challenged to remain tenderhearted and thick-skinned; to be kind, gentle, and trusting, while rejected, dismissed, and overwhelmed. The only way we can love and wait well under these circumstances is to keep our hearts fixed on Jesus.

Christ-centered stepmothering invites constriction, but the juice is worth the squeeze. I want the joy of pleasing God, the thrill of becoming more like Jesus, and the contentment I find resting in His ability to change hearts, more than the momentary pleasure of doing things my way. In the topsy-turvy, upside down lifestyle that is living in the Kingdom of God, Christlikeness is an invitation to die to self, yet come alive to the best you possible. Loving before being loved will bless your spiritual formation in amazing ways.

Loving before being loved prompts a receptivity to the Holy Spirit's work in our hearts. As you wait, He plants, water, and grows His fruit, love, joy, peace, patience, kindness, goodness, faithfulness, gentleness, and self-control. As you wait, He leads, comforts, encourages, and strengthens you. The fact that He lives in you is the guarantee of the finished and complete work of Christ. He points you to Christ. He uses you to point others to Christ. He dispenses the love of God into your heart and causes it to overflow into the lives of others. Through the work of the Holy Spirit, you become the catalyst through which your family is blessed.

Waiting is complicated. It's a jumbled process in which you're okay one moment and triggered into a meltdown the next. The concept of waiting is simple. It's merely the interval of time between what we have and what we want. Clear. Easy. Understandable. Nonetheless, waiting is messy in its application. Waiting does not come in a neat package tied up with a bow. There are stages without sequence. We need the Lord as we walk this road. We need His help to survive the in between. Praise God, we have it!

The Playing the Waiting Game chapter in Waiting to be Wanted talks about stages to waiting. Take a moment to reread the definitions and determine where you are:

- ◊ Hope
- ◊ Fantasizing
- ◊ Doubting
- ◊ Rationalization
- ◊ Frustration
- ◊ Resentment
- ◊ Anger
- ◊ Self-pity
- ◊ Acceptance
- ◊ Relief

Our prayer is that by the time you get to the end of Waiting to be Wanted, and this companion workbook, you will be one step further than you are today.

SECTION I

The Famished Heart

Lord, save me from myself

"I will refresh the weary and satisfy the faint."

Jeremiah 31:25

God never leaves us *deprived.*

MALNOURISHED MOMS

Jesus puts importance on being childlike. Not in how we think, or engage the world, but how we relate to our Heavenly Father. It is difficult to maintain childlikeness in a world that puts non-childlike pressure on our hearts.

What child-like traits are present in your walk with Christ? (trust, curiosity, generosity, acceptance, innocence faith, contentment, obedience, etc.)

_____
_____
_____
_____
_____

Which ones are missing?

_____
_____
_____
_____
_____

HOW NOURISHED IS YOUR HEART?

Sometimes it is hard to know if we're living with emaciated hearts. We become functional carcasses: taking care of the business of the day yet dying inside. Take a moment to diagnose the degree of malnourishment you may be experiencing.

How physically exhausted are you?
1   2   3   4   5   6   7
No energy at all.   Raring to go!

Are you more easily irritated than usual?
1   2   3   4   5   6   7
Don't touch me!   I love people.

How well are you sleeping?
1　　　2　　　3　　　4　　　5　　　6　　　7
What's sleep?　　　　　　　　　　　　　　　　8 hours a night.

Do you have a circle of friends upon whom you rely?
1　　　2　　　3　　　4　　　5　　　6　　　7
I trust no one.　　　　　　　　　　　　　　　　My tribe rocks!

Are you short-tempered, yelling at people?
1　　　2　　　3　　　4　　　5　　　6　　　7
They get on my nerves!　　　　　　　　　　　　Only, "Yeah!"

How vibrant is your devotional time with the Lord?
1　　　2　　　3　　　4　　　5　　　6　　　7
Robotic, when I get to it.　　　　　　　　　　　Best time of day.

How are you managing challenging circumstances?
1　　　2　　　3　　　4　　　5　　　6　　　7
I cry every night.　　　　　　　　　　　　　　Cool and steady.

Do you schedule time for activities you enjoy?
1　　　2　　　3　　　4　　　5　　　6　　　7
Don't have time to blink.　　　　　　　　　　　Every week.

If you are on the low end of the spectrum for three or more of these, you may have a heart in need of special attention.

Take a moment to jot down some ways in which you can nourish your heart (i.e., spend regular time with the Lord, set aside time for a favorite hobby, regular phone call with a friend, etc.):

_____
_____
_____
_____
_____
_____
_____

Agape is so other focused, there is no room for self-protection.

A HEART IN HIDING

Janie swallowed the hurt. By now it was habit. Janie never asked for what she needed. For the life of her, she couldn't understand why no one could see that she, too, required support. She did so much for the people around her, stepchildren included. All she asked for was a little consideration. So, Janie swallowed, and stuffed, and silenced her voice. Until she could take it no longer, then she exploded in, what seemed to her family, unreasonable anger. Feeling ashamed, she silenced her voice again.

DO YOU STRUGGLE WITH A HIDDEN HEART?

Janie was afraid to ask for what she needed for fear of being seen as a demanding woman. She relied on her family intuiting what she needed by demonstrating behavior she wanted reciprocated. Unfortunately, they did not get the message, which caused Janie to feel resentful and angry. It took a couple years, and the mastery of new communication skills, for Janie to uncloak her heart.

How you come out of hiding will depend on a few things:

What's cloaking your heart? Is it fear? Childhood trauma? Abandonment? Rejection?

_____
_____
_____
_____
_____

**Somethings will need the expertise of a therapist or pastor trained in trauma.

How hidden is your heart? Are you very self-aware but choosing to remain closed off? Do you have a hard time identifying your feelings? Distinguishing between perspective and truth?

_____
_____
_____

_____
_____

Think of a recurring situation in your family which causes you stress. Ask yourself these questions:

Why is this bothering me

_____
_____
_____
_____
_____

What memory is this triggering?

_____
_____
_____
_____
_____

What learned behaviors are you using to protect your heart? Sarcasm? Put-downs? Self-deprecation? Notice what makes you uncomfortable and what you do to deflect that unrest.

_____
_____
_____
_____
_____

How often is your heart assaulted? Are you living in a constant battleground? Is it seasonal? Usually related to special events or holidays?

_____
_____
_____

_____
_____

The first step in learning how to love before being loved is to bring that heart out of hiding. My own journey led me to a few discoveries:

- ◊ The more open you are, the more likely you'll get hurt, but it's way better than remaining isolated within relationships.

- ◊ God is a better protector of our heart than we could ever hope to be. When it gets stung, and yes, that will happen, we can take that pain, discouragement, and upset, right to Abba. He will comfort us.

- ◊ We won't always feel affectionate, but it's important we keep doing love. The emotions will catch up at some point.

- ◊ Eventually fear loses its grip. Apostle John reminds us in 1 John 4 there is no fear in love for perfect love drives out fear (1 John 4:18). Keep your heart accessible to the people in your life while God is working in it. Fear will go.

- ◊ We don't have to rely on our own reservoir of love. The love of God, 1st Corinthians 13 love, has been poured into our hearts by the Holy Spirit (Romans 5:5). When our emotional tanks are running on empty, the Holy Spirit will refill and strengthen us.

- ◊ As you uncover your heart, God does the work of recovering it. He heals, redeems, restores, and writes truth upon your heart.

Which of the listed discoveries surprise you? Inspire hope?

_____
_____
_____
_____
_____

In what ways?

_____
_____
_____
_____
_____

Perhaps you have done the work of bringing your heart out of hiding. What other discoveries have you made?

_____
_____
_____
_____
_____
_____
_____
_____
_____
_____
_____

During my divorce, my heart was in danger of running further into hiding. Like any other person going through a painful situation, I felt alone, unseen, and unheard; until I took the brave step of opening up to the Lord and the people, He sent to help me. I did not get what I wanted initially: the restoration of my marriage. Nevertheless, by the time my marriage dissolved, God's nearness comforted, contented, and encouraged me to such a great extent, the demise of the marriage was anticlimactic. My only regret was the pain my daughter experienced. However, God even brought good out of that. The phone rang one chilly October evening. Kayla was on the other end of the line. She began describing her heartache for a friend who was having a hard time with her father. Because of what Kayla experienced, she was able to empathize and pray for her friend. Tears pooled in my eyes when Kayla said, "You know, Mom. I hate what happened with Dad but I'm so glad I can be there for my friend." God's faithfulness encourages open-hearted living.

FOR FURTHER STUDY

Read Genesis 37-50

Note each time Joseph faced a dream-deferring detour.

_____
_____
_____
_____

How did Joseph respond?

_____
_____
_____
_____

What detours have you experienced?

_____
_____
_____
_____

How did your response differ from Joseph's?

_____
_____
_____
_____

What good did God bring from the evil your antagonist meant?

_____
_____
_____

TREASURE HUNT

1 Thessalonians 2:7-8 reads: Instead, we were like young children among you. Just as a nursing mother cares for her children, so we cared for you. Because we loved you so much, we were delighted to share with you not only the gospel of God but our lives as well. (NIV).

We glean a deeper meaning from the Amplified Classic translation: But we behaved gently when we were among you, like a devoted mother nursing and cherishing her own children. So, being thus tenderly and affectionately desirous of you, we continued to share with you not only God's good news (the Gospel) but also our own lives as well, for you had become so very dear to us.

How does your heart attitude toward the children gifted to you through marriage compare to that of Paul's towards the Thessalonians?

_____
_____
_____
_____
_____

What is God revealing to you about your thoughts towards your bonus children? In what ways are your thoughts pleasing to Him?

_____
_____
_____
_____
_____
_____

Write out a prayer asking God to give you His eternal perspective on your role in your family. Ask Him to work love and affection for your family into your heart, so that you can give them both the Gospel and yourself. Trust that He will complete this work in you.

Our fight to *love,* while we are *waiting* to be loved, is also a fight *against* the enemy!

SHARK BAIT

One more snide comment and I was going to snap. We were in the hospital in an emergency situation. Kayla was less than 3 months old, running a temperature of 103.5 and the doctors could not figure out what was wrong. They could not get her fever under control and decided to do a spinal tap to check for meningitis. I was terrified. They ushered her dad and me out of the room so they could perform the procedure without the presence of gasping and grasping parents. In the waiting room sat my mother, my former mother-in-law, and Kayla's godparents. As soon as we sat down, she began needling, turning to Kayla's godfather, "Maybe this will make a man out of him. You know I always wished my son had married a woman like your wife." On and on she went, while her granddaughter was getting a needle stuck into her spine. My former mother-in-law was a divisive person, to put it mildly. The night of Kay's spinal tap she was in rare form. I remember thinking, "If she doesn't shut up, I'm going to shut her up!" God used the wisdom of Kayla's godfather to save me from taking the bait and stepping into that trap. He simply turned away from her and said, "Let's pray."

I was ready to walk right into the trap Satan used my former mother-in-law to set for me. It was during a particularly vulnerable moment. Our vigilance is compromised in stressful situations. It is one of the most strategic times to strike.

When has offense trapped you into sin?

_____
_____
_____
_____

In the book, Samantha had several "tells" which alerted her friend to the offense lodged in her heart. List the ones you notice:

_____
_____
_____
_____

Are any of these apparent in your actions and attitudes? If so, which ones?

_____
_____
_____
_____
_____

Our fight to love while we're waiting to be loved is also a fight against the enemy. Against his tactics. Against deception. Against his plans for our loved ones. Against the lies he spins and the division he pitches at our families. Against the poison of offense.

5 ACTIONS TO GUARD AGAINST OFFENSE

- ◊ Typically, offense comes when we're triggered in a place of woundedness. Someone has shaken our broken place and we're screaming. Unfortunately, we often don't know what our wounds are or how they occurred. Take time to discover your story. Ask Jesus to help you see what wounds you may have and how they affect your ability to deal with offenses. If needed, enlist the help of your pastor or a good therapist to gain insight and healing.

- ◊ Shhh! Stop fighting. Tear down your walls but keep your fences. Maintain healthy boundaries. Walls separate. In every way. Healthy boundaries, however, are the physical, emotional and mental limits we establish to protect ourselves from being manipulated, used, or violated by others while remaining open to them. They allow us to separate who we are, and what we think and feel, from the thoughts and feelings of others. The presence of healthy boundaries helps us express ourselves as the unique individuals we are, while we acknowledge and esteem the same in others.

- ◊ Determine beforehand to avoid the boxing ring. Proverbs 26:21 tells us: Just as charcoal and wood keep a fire going, a quarrelsome person keeps an argument going. Offense needs fuel to reach maximum effectiveness. Don't feed the opportunities. As much as it depends on you, walk in peace with all men. (Romans 12:18) Attack issues, not your stepchildren. Correct behavior without arguing about perspective.

- ◊ Manage your expectations so you can apply pressure in the appropriate place. There is a huge difference between good desires and lust. We were made for relationship with others. That is a good desire given to us by God. However, relationships with others were not made to fill all of our relational needs. To demand, or even expect someone to fulfill our relational longings, is lust and a form of idolatry. Only God can do that. Look to the Father for the deeper needs of acceptance, validation, identity, security, and emotional healing. This will make it easier for you to love the people in your life without pressuring them to love you in return and feeling offended when they cannot.

- ◊ I cannot stress this action step enough: spend time worshipping God. Maintaining a proper view of God will help you maintain a proper view of who you are. When we consider that a Holy God, without sin or stain, who is just in His offense at our sin, rather than punish us, removes our sin through the precious blood of Jesus, it becomes much easier to forgive the offenses of one sinner against another. That does not mean it will be effortless, but it becomes easier when we realize how much we owe God.

Which one of these actions is the Holy Spirit asking you to take? How can you implement the step outlined?

_____
_____
_____
_____

Read the following Scriptures:

    1 Peter 1:6-7

    1 Peter 2:19-25

What do these scriptures tell us that will help us further guard against offense?

_____
_____
_____
_____
_____

No matter how adept we became at guarding against offense, it will burst through those defenses at some point. I had to learn what to do when offended. If you are wondering how to reclaim peace when offended, I have something which may help:

5 ACTIONS TO RECOVER FROM OFFENSE

- ◊ Acknowledge your feelings. In the Scriptures we read in Luke 17, Jesus' instructions to us were: "…If your brother sins against you, rebuke him…" Recovering from offense in no way means denying you've been hurt. We're encouraged by Jesus to go to our "brother" (or sister, or husband, or whomever) and LOVINGLY rebuke their actions, in order to bring about reconciliation. Hurt feelings will not diminish with denial. They will only grow stronger. Deal with them quickly.

- ◊ Proverbs 19:11 reads: A man's wisdom gives him patience. It is to his glory to overlook an offense. Offense provides an opportunity for us to grow into greater glory. God does not waste anything. Offense is a tool for spiritual training. As we focus on His faithfulness rather than our hurt, God uses offense for our good: to change us to look, think, and act, more and more like Jesus. Give Him access to your heart when offended. He will help you overlook offense, causing you to mature in Christ.

- ◊ Don't wait for an apology. It may never come. Choose to forgive. Jesus was asked the Father to forgive his executioners while He was dying. (Luke 23:34) Paul reminds us in Colossians: You must make allowance for each other's faults and forgive the person who offends you. Remember the Lord forgave you, so you must forgive others. (Col 3:13) Holding on to an offense keeps you shackled to the wound, sets the stage for bitterness to take root in your heart, and, according to the Bible, results in God withholding His forgiveness (Matthew 6:15). Free yourself. Do not wait for relief or good feelings to return. Make allowances for others and choose forgiveness as often as you need to.

- ◊ Paul wrote to the Corinthians: You even put up with anyone who enslaves you or exploits you or takes advantage of you or pushes himself forward or slaps you in the face (2 Corinthians 11:20). As much as possible, remove yourself from repeat offenders. Value what God values. God values both you and the person who has hurt you. He values peace and unity. He values your family. He values justice. Removing yourself will give you the needed space to determine how to respond. Distance makes it easier to recover from offense through prayer and a renewed perspective. Ask yourself: "Am I able to remain in relationship with the person and not act in sinful ways towards them because of their actions against me?" If not, step away.

- ◊ Pray. Repeatedly. Forgiveness doesn't happen in one fell swoop; don't stop praying until you have totally forgiven the offender. Bring your authentic self to your time of prayer. I confess to God when it is hard for me to forgive, and I ask Him to help me obey Him. He always helps when we cry out to Him for assistance. Make sure, after you have prayed for yourself, pray for the person who has offended you. Ask God to bless them. Pray for those you have offended. Ask God to remove the sting of offense and help them recover well.

Which one of these actions is the Holy Spirit asking you to take? How can you implement the step outlined?

_____
_____
_____
_____
_____

TREASURE HUNT

"But you, O Sovereign Lord, deal well with me for your name's sake; out of the goodness of your love, deliver me. For I am poor and needy, and my heart is wounded within me." Psalm 109: 21-22 NIV

Think about an incident where you were particularly hurt by the words or actions of your stepchild. Use the space provided to write it out.

_____
_____
_____
_____
_____

Take a moment to pray and ask Jesus to reveal deeper truths about yourself in context of your hurt. Ask yourself the following questions:

What hurtful feelings were stirred?

_____
_____
_____
_____
_____

What past experiences do I associate with those feelings? What wounds were touched?

_____
_____
_____
_____
_____

What lies do I believe about myself because of those wounds?

_____
_____
_____
_____
_____

How did these past experiences shape my response to my stepchild?

_____
_____
_____
_____
_____

How might God be using this incident to help me live unoffended?

_____
_____
_____
_____
_____

Now spend time in prayer over your discoveries. Ask Jesus to give you the truth to combat every lie you believe. Use this space to record His scriptures, or answers:

_____
_____
_____
_____
_____

Hope turns a *worrier* into a *Warrior!*

HOPE DEFERRED

"I am looking forward to when they are true friends," Cathy lamented. Cathy, and her husband, Frank, have a blended family of four children. Although each child got along quite well with their respective stepparent, they do not get along with each other. A "them vs. us" line had been drawn and no one wanted to be the first to cross it. Both Cathy and Frank think well of all of the children. They prayed the children would think well of each other and begin to turn to each other for friendship and support. It seemed as if their hope for a bonded family was ill-founded. But, their hope was not in their children; it was in God. He specializes in things which seem impossible.

LIVING HOPE

The Hebrew word for "hope" is yachal. It means to have a confident expectation, usually accompanied by pleasurable anticipation. Biblical hope is closer to faith than it is wishing.

"I am so convinced of the inevitable goodness of God being revealed in my life, I live in constant anticipation of that good, despite what I see going on around me!"

What unrealized hopes for your family are you living with today?

_____
_____
_____
_____
_____

FOR FURTHER STUDY

Read Numbers 13 – 14

God instructs Moses to send twelve spies into the "Promised Land" on a recon mission. When the spies return, they tell Moses and the people of Israel, "we went into the land where you sent us; and it certainly does flow with milk and honey" (Numbers 13:27).

Each of the twelve spies saw the Promised Land. But, there was a difference in attitude among them. Joshua and Caleb counseled the people to move forward. They had faith in God, and knew, with Him, they would be successful. For the rest of the spies, their inadequacies eclipsed God's sufficiency. They said, "We are not able to go up against the people for they are too strong for us" (Numbers 13:31). Unfortunately, the people of Israel followed the naysayers.

As you consider the two different responses God received from His people, answer the questions below:

What promises of God for your family are you struggling with believing?
___
___
___
___
___

How are the dynamics in your family feeding hope or shrinking faith?

___
___
___
___
___

If the things that shake your faith has captured your attention, how can you shift your focus back to God's promises?

___
___
___
___
___

Joshua and Caleb had each other. Name the strong-in-faith friends you can call on to help you maintain a habit of hope:

___ __

_____
_____
_____
_____
_____

YOUR WELLS

Jesus reached out to the woman at the well with Living Water. His intention was to satisfy her true need. He saw her. He knew her. His eyes held welcome and redemption. He says to you what He said to her, "I already know."

What "old wells" have you revisited? What have you looked to, other than Jesus, to ease the heartsickness of hope deferred?

_____
_____
_____
_____
_____

What truth have you discovered that will dry up those insufficient wells?

_____
_____
_____
_____
_____

Our scripture for this chapter is Proverbs 13:12:

> *Hope deferred makes the heart sick, but a longing fulfilled is a tree of life.*

Remembrances of God's past faithfulness ignites hope for His continued faithfulness.

What longings has God fulfilled for you?

_____
_____
_____
_____
_____
_____

I prayed Romans 15:13 for you. Use this space to record a prayer thanking God for filling your heart with hope:

_____
_____
_____
_____
_____
_____

TREASURE HUNT

Take a doubt inventory in your life.

What key points of doubt have taken hold of your relationship with your stepchildren?

_____
_____
_____
_____

Where is the doubting attitude evident in your actions and reactions?

_____
_____
_____
_____

Read Psalm 48:14. How does knowing God will guide you until the end feed your hope?

_____

_____
_____
_____
_____
_____

What are the consequences of the doubts you experience? Focus on the emotional, physical and spiritual areas of your life.

_____
_____
_____
_____
_____

What scriptures will help you replace a doubting attitude with biblical hope?

1. Scripture: _____
   _____
   _____
   _____

2. Scripture: _____
   _____
   _____
   _____

3. Scripture: _____
   _____
   _____
   _____

4. Scripture: _____
   _____
   _____
   _____

Some *agitation* is good for the *Soul!*

CAN I GET OFF NOW?

Theresa stood in the school gym with her husband, his daughter, and his ex-wife. They were waiting as Theresa's stepdaughter received congratulations after a stellar performance. Jesse introduced her mom, and her dad to her well-wishers. Once again, she ignored Theresa. Why was it every time bio-mom was around, Jesse mistreated her? She understood conflict of loyalties, but a little courtesy wasn't too much to ask, was it? She was seriously contemplating not coming to these events anymore, but what would that communicate?

Theresa was caught in a pretty typical blended family drama, but she was tired of it. Her struggle over whether or not to attend anymore events, where she might be relegated to stagehand status, was her first step away from home. Theresa isn't alone in her stepmomma angst.

What is driving you away from home? What issues keep you on an emotional rollercoaster, clamoring for an exit strategy?

_____
_____
_____
_____
_____

How many outings have you dreaded because you didn't know what type of ride you were waiting in line for? How many times have you asked, "are we climbing or plummeting?" You were built for the excitement, joy, and turbulence of the life you're living. No matter how many ups and downs your heart experiences, God has equipped you to withstand the agitation.

Read Colossians 1:9-11

It is God's will for you to walk worthy of Him, bear good fruit, and be strengthened by His Spirit. Tell a story of a time when you knew God had strengthened you for the task ahead of you:

_____

_____
_____
_____
_____

Use this space to write out Hebrews 10:36:

_____
_____
_____

God always has goodness in store for you and your family, but to experience the goodness you have to suffer the not so good.

What helps you persevere the dips in blended family life, so that you can receive God's promise?

_____
_____
_____
_____
_____

What can you no longer tolerate?

_____
_____
_____
_____
_____

What one thing could be added, or removed, to help you withstand the ride?

_____
_____
_____
_____
_____

I am challenged to approach life in my stepfamily with the same degree of thrilled anticipation as I do while in line to ride a rollercoaster; knowing I will experience the peaks of joy and valleys of heartache, but not knowing when. Perhaps, our struggle with the unknown is purposeful. Some agitation is good for the soul.

How might God be using the agitations in your blended family for your good?

_____
_____
_____
_____
_____

Our "downs" on this ride can feel like failures and missteps. But they qualify us for help and aid from the Holy Spirit. They also qualify us to empathize and guide. How have the downs served you? Your family? Others?

_____
_____
_____
_____
_____

As we are learning to hang on, there are ways in which we cooperate with the work of grace in our lives, and maintain a balanced sense of well-being, peace, and hope while we experience the ups and downs:

- ◊ Make no rash decisions. Think twice before acting.

- ◊ Spend time with friends or in activities that feed your soul.

- ◊ Trust God to provide a well-spring in the desert.

- ◊ Rehearse your God stories.

- ◊ But don't ignore the struggles you've been facing.

- ◊ Forgive your family members for the words and actions which sent you hurtling towards the ground at top speed.

- ◊ Harness the negative thoughts that make you want to quit and replace them with God's truth.

- ◊ Don't ride alone.

What stands out to you? Why?

_____
_____
_____
_____
_____

TREASURE HUNT

Reread the list of ways in which we can cooperate with the work of God's grace to maintain stability on this rollercoaster of a ride we call living in-step.

Which two actions are you going to take?

_____
_____
_____
_____
_____

Why did you choose those specific actions?

_____
_____

How will incorporating these actions serve you as a stepmom?

What changes do you need to make?

Now spend some time in prayer, asking God to help you remain emotionally steady in your family, to anchor you in His word, and to help you as you lean on His strength to embody the actions you're taking. Record any insights, scriptures, or words of encouragement you get during your time in prayer.

Defined *intentions* are *reached* intentions.

THRIVER IN HIDING

Sometimes the best solution lies in how the Holy Spirit changes our hearts, versus how our circumstances change. Let's explore the possibility of inward transformation to bring about outward change.

Name one specific area in which you want to see progress in your stepmom/stepchild relationship:

_____
_____
_____
_____
_____

What could change about you that would affect this situation?

_____
_____
_____
_____
_____

Paul wrote in Romans: *"We glory in tribulations: knowing that tribulation worketh patience; and patience, experience; and experience, hope…"* (Romans 5:3-4). Let's assume God designed your relational struggle to transform you. What's the opportunity here?

_____
_____
_____
_____
_____

When we face a challenge, we are either broken by it, survive it, or it becomes a defining moment. What response would make the challenges you face in your family a defining moment for you?

_____
_____
_____
_____
_____
_____

What internal obstacles are keeping you from moving forward? What would it take for these obstacles to be gone?

_____
_____
_____
_____
_____
_____

List scripture(s) to help this become the moment in which you begin to turn the corner in this struggle:

1. Scripture: _____
   _____
   _____
   _____

2. Scripture: _____
   _____
   _____
   _____

3. Scripture: _____
   _____
   _____
   _____

4. Scripture: _____
   _____
   _____
   _____

EMOTIONAL VOCABULARY

Once, while chatting with Jonathan about my role as a stepmom, I said, "I feel like I'm not seen." He gave me a blank stare as he tried to figure out what I was telling him. I thought I told him I felt hurt, sad, defeated, and uncertain. He was frustrated by hearing a problem to fix but not understanding the issue. Classic communication misfire.

Emotions inform our choices, frame memories, and send messages, but most of us have a limited repertoire of words to describe our emotional state. Difficulty in identifying and expressing emotion is common, yet it is a critical skill to learn. Especially if we want honest connection with the people around us.

This exercise will help you build your emotional vocabulary. I learned a few tips from Nonviolent Communication by Marshall B. Rosenberg which will assist you:

1. Distinguish feelings from thoughts. Avoid phrases like; I feel like..., I feel as if..., I feel you..., I feel she.... I feel Margaret...

2. Distinguish between what we feel and what we think we are. For example, assessing ability (I feel inadequate as a stepmom) vs. an actual feeling (I am frustrated with myself as a stepmom.)

3. Distinguish between what we feel and how we think others react or behave toward us. For example, saying, "I feel unwanted by my stepchildren" vs. saying, "I am pained by the state of my relationship with my stepchildren."

Practice: Your stepdaughter calls you, for the first time, just to chat about her day. What words can you use to express your feelings (i.e.: happy, excited, fascinated, etc.)? Write out a sentence using the feeling words you've chosen:

_____
_____
_____

For this exercise, we are going to practice using "feeling" words to express emotions:

Use the space provided to record how you feel about your stepmothering role. Use the principles discussed above:

_____
_____
_____
_____
_____

Note: If you'd like feedback on how well your response expressed feelings, please feel free to email us at info@stepmomsanity.com. Use "Feedback on Feeling Exercise" as the subject line.

Rosenbberg, Phd., Marshall B. Nonviolent Communication: A Language of Life, Encintas: Puddle Dancer Press, 2015. Print

SCRIPTURE MEDITATION

Turn to the Prune Your Heart chapter in your book. Use the lines below to record, and answer questions for, three of the scriptures on which the Holy Spirit focuses your attention.

Scripture reference: _____
Written Scripture
_____
_____
_____
_____
_____

How is the Holy Spirit encouraging me through this scripture?

_____
_____
_____
_____
_____
_____

How is the Holy Spirit challenging me through this scripture?

_____
_____
_____
_____
_____
_____

Scripture reference: _____
Written Scripture

_____
_____
_____
_____
_____

How is the Holy Spirit encouraging me through this scripture?

_____
_____
_____
_____
_____
_____

How is the Holy Spirit challenging me through this scripture?

_____
_____
_____
_____
_____
_____

Scripture reference: _____
Written Scripture

_____
_____
_____
_____
_____
_____

How is the Holy Spirit encouraging me through this scripture?

_____
_____
_____
_____
_____
_____

How is the Holy Spirit challenging me through this scripture?

_____
_____
_____
_____
_____
_____

What other observations have I made?

_____
_____
_____
_____
_____

SECTION I NOTES

SECTION II

The Focused Heart

Lord, fill me with more of you!

"Let us not become weary in doing good, for at the proper time we will reap a harvest if we do not give up."

Galatians 6:9

We do what we do *because* we love *God.*

MEASURED MOMS

Our "why" will energize us. Our "why" will prop up tenacity. Methods, strategies, and blueprints give us a roadmap but without a compelling "why," our "want to" will fizzle out. God wants more than invitation into our struggles. He wants more than robotic obedience. God wants a deep surrender to Him in our step-mothering so that we reflect His steady love and overwhelming goodness to our families. He wants a relationship. One that includes heart to heart encounters with Him, in which we fall to our knees in worship, and rise in love-sick, awe-struck obedience.

Glorifying Him in all I do has become my "why". Our relationship with God is not defined by either a list of "to don'ts" or "to dos." "Should" has no right to invade our relationship with God. We do what we do because we love God.

Let's take a moment to explore ways in which dispensing with "should" frees us to follow the steady rhythm of grace.

Make a list of "I should" or "we should" statements that have put pressure on your role and/or your family. (i.e., I should think this way. I should be feeling that way. My family should...)

_____
_____
_____
_____
_____

"I should" leads to struggle and disappointment. Grace leads to acceptance and peace. List more grace-filled patterns of thinking that can replace "I should"?

_____
_____
_____
_____
_____

The litmus test for success as a stepmom is her own response to God's direction.

THE FOCUSED HEART

What does this statement mean to you?

_____
_____
_____
_____
_____

What's motivating you right now?

_____
_____
_____
_____
_____

What legacy do you want to leave for your family?

_____
_____
_____
_____
_____

Freedom and Wholeness await you.

SPARKED

Susan was stunted by her father's rejection. I was stunted by my peers'. The enemy is skilled at using the broken people around us to threaten our precious identities. However, God is a deliverer. He is able to mend our broken places and restore them with grace and glory.

How would you love differently if you knew those broken places, broken people, and lies had no more power over you?

_____
_____
_____
_____
_____

We will be able to love, without being loved, when we remain aware of God's goodness and faithfulness. We will only recognize and receive God's goodness and faithfulness when we're convinced of God's love. The best way to be convinced of His goodness today is to remember, rehearse, and celebrate His past goodness.

In what ways has God's restoration convinced you of His love?

_____
_____
_____
_____
_____

Write your goodness psalm:

_____, His love endures forever!

_____, His love endures forever!

_____, His love endures forever!

_____, His love endures forever!

_____, His love endures forever!

_____, His love endures forever!

_____, His love endures forever!

Laurie's friend prayed for her:

"Laurie. Your heart is so ugly right now, but God wants to set you free. He wants to use you to reach your stepdaughter but you're so in love with yourself and your needs and your hurts, you can't see beyond you. His desire is for us to be like Him in the way He loves. That's what Jesus commanded, that we would love others in the way Jesus loves us. This is how He loves us, Laurie.

While we were His enemies, He died for you, for me, for your stepdaughter. Jesus didn't wait for us to act a certain way, to love Him, or even like Him. He loved us because that's who He is. And that's the kind of love He has placed in our hearts through His precious Holy Spirit. Love that will see your stepdaughter's pain, see her need, see her worth and respond because she's more important to you than you are. That's the love He will empower you to show your stepdaughter...the same kind He has shown to you."

Do her words convict you? If so, how? How do her words affirm or convict you?

_____
_____
_____
_____
_____

What one thing do you think you need to walk in the love of God?

_____
_____
_____
_____
_____

LOVE MADE KNOWN

God made His love known to me while I sat completely in love with my newborn daughter. How has God made His love known to you, outside of Calvary?

_____
_____
_____
_____
_____

1 John 4:7-11 reads:

Dear friends, let us love one another, for love comes from God. Everyone who loves has been born of God and knows God.

Whoever does not love does not know God, because God is love.

This is how God showed his love among us: He sent his one and only Son into the world that we might live through him.

This is love: not that we loved God, but that he loved us and sent his Son as an atoning sacrifice for our sins.

Dear friends, since God so loved us, we also ought to love one another.

Write out our declaration of identity from the book:

"I _____ the _____

whom God _____!"

God's love is in you. You have the ability to show His love. Knowing that you don't have to conjure up love frees you to be daring. Write out your dangerous "Jesus, help me love like You" prayer:

_____

THE FOCUSED HEART

TREASURE HUNT

1 Corinthians 13:4-8 paints the picture of what agape looks like applied to everyday life. Take a moment to prayerfully read the scriptures. As you read, note the times God has been patient with you, kind to you, took pleasure in your accomplishments, saw to your needs, etc.

Thank God for the perceptible expression of His love:

How would you apply the characteristics of agape to your stepparenting?

Patience
_____
_____

Kind
_____
_____

Not Jealous
_____
_____

Humble
_____
_____

Unpretentious
_____
_____

Honoring
_____
_____

Agreeable
_____
_____

Forgiving
_____
_____

Does not delight in wrongdoing
_____
_____

Rejoices in truth
_____
_____

Protective
_____
_____

Trusting
_____
_____

Hopeful
_____
_____

Perseveres
_____
_____

God commits His *power* to assist our *surrender.*

THE (HE)ART OF RENEGOTIATION

By the grace of God, empathy served Paul for the sake of the gospel. Likewise, empathy serves us in our families. Where can you incorporate more empathy in your stepmothering?

_____
_____
_____
_____
_____

THE THRONE OF YOUR LIFE

Patrice stood in the doorway, watching Thomas drive away. This time, he didn't come in. He sat in the car for five minutes, with head bowed. He looked up, saw Patrice standing at the door, then backed out of the driveway. Patrice closed the door and turned to face the chaos in her home alone. Thomas and Patrice had been married for 15 years. They were locked in a battle over how to care for a terminal parent. At the same time, Patrice had reignited a relationship with an old boyfriend from college. Thomas had no clue. He only knew something was terribly wrong and he didn't know how to fix it. Rather than genuinely turn to the Lord, Patrice continued the relationship with her ex-boyfriend, and Thomas continued to neglect his home. Patrice resisted God's clear direction to stop the relationship. Thomas resisted God's direction to be there for his family. They both resisted God's instructions to submit to one another, pray for each other, forgive and restore each other.

Read the scriptures below:

> *Know that the Lord, he is God! It is he who made us, and we are his; we are his people, and the sheep of his pasture.*
> Psalm 100:3

> *But now thus says the Lord, he who created you, O Jacob, he who formed you, O Israel: "Fear not, for I have redeemed you; I have called you by name, you are mine.*
> Isaiah 43:1

For if we live, we live to the Lord, and if we die, we die to the Lord. So then, whether we live or whether we die, we are the Lord's.
Romans 14:8

I have been crucified with Christ. It is no longer I who live, but Christ who lives in me. And the life I now live in the flesh I live by faith in the Son of God, who loved me and gave himself for me.
Galatians 2:20

You were bought with a price; do not become slaves of men.
1 Corinthians 7:23

God owns us, entirely, completely, and supremely. We are indebted to Him. Redemption compels our obedience, service, and fidelity to Jesus. Not in a tyrannical bid for submission. Obedience, service, and fidelity has been lovingly curated by the sacrificing King, whose every decision brings us into a deeper, more tangible experience of abundant life. However, any resistance to His will or direction is rebellion. Rebellion has its outcomes as well.

What might you miss by allowing your emotions to dictate your actions and reactions?

_____
_____
_____
_____
_____

DEALING WITH THE EMOTIONS

Our hearts have no bargaining position when it comes to obeying God. We either obey Him or not.

What emotions are you wrestling with the most?

_____
_____
_____

_____
_____
_____

In renegotiation we must unload the burden until the issue is simplified. What haven't you said to the Lord?

_____
_____
_____
_____
_____

When you're renegotiating with your heart, you will need to walk it out with a trusted someone. Who's on your team?

_____
_____
_____
_____
_____

RESOLUTE

Jesus acknowledged the battle in His flesh but refused to allow His flesh to dictate His obedience. He had made up His mind.

What feeds your resolve to obey the Lord in your stepmothering?

_____
_____
_____
_____
_____

Robert Murray M'Cheyne, a 19th-century Scottish minister, said, "If I could hear Christ praying for me in the next room, I would not fear a million enemies. Yet the distance makes no difference; He is praying for me!"

Write out Isaiah 50:7

_____
_____
_____
_____
_____

Why is it important to know Jesus is praying for us and the Sovereign Lord will help us?

_____
_____
_____
_____
_____

TREASURE HUNT

What one issue in your stepmom life causes your heart to disengage?

_____
_____
_____
_____
_____

What is the constant dripping, in your thinking, that wears away at your intention to love your stepchildren before you are loved by them?

_____
_____
_____
_____
_____

We undermine God's authority when we redefine His instructions to us. Where are you struggling with obedience to God regarding your stepmomming?

_____
_____
_____
_____
_____

Now, carve out some time, grab your bible, your journal, a pen, and find a quiet space where you can wrestle with God in your own "Garden of Gethsemane." Unburden yourself. Lay it all down. Don't go in with a heart to convince God of something against His word. Go with a mind to bring your heart into alignment with His will. Allow His truth to mold your heart. Ask for His Holy Spirit to help and strengthen you.

Letting go gives our *hearts* permission to *Thrive!*

SACRED STRATEGIES

Jenni stubbornly held on to the intent in her heart. It was the day before Mother's Day, and her stepdaughter had asked that they all go out to dinner, rather than split time. It was nice of her but perhaps not very wise. The melee began about half-way through dinner. Jenni had made up her mind before dinner started that she was not going to be pushed around today. Bio-mom began needling. Jenni sighed. She silently prayed. The Lord impressed, "Be silent," upon her heart. Jenni was tired of being an easy punching bag. She opened her mouth and poured gas on the fire.

Has your "mind" ever told you to go a different direction than God instructed?

_____
_____
_____
_____
_____

How did that work out for you?

_____
_____
_____
_____
_____

How were you able to recover?

_____
_____
_____
_____
_____

Recall a time when you followed the Lord. How was the outcome different than when you followed your own mind?

_____
_____

THE FOCUSED HEART

_____
_____
_____

What are some of the benefits we gain by immediate obedience to God (i.e.: peace, protection, etc.)?

_____
_____
_____
_____
_____

Are there any strategies you have been given for interacting with your family?

_____
_____
_____
_____
_____

TREASURE HUNT

We discussed the strategies the Lord gave to me for interacting with my family. They are:

1. Approach with humility
2. Approach ready to serve
3. Approach with the end in mind
4. Approach to understand
5. Approach looking for the win
6. Approach with honor
7. Approach with baby steps
8. Approach with deodorizer
9. Approach with an open hand
10. Approach with expectation

Which strategies stand out to you?

_____
_____
_____
_____
_____

Find two scriptures to support the main theme of each strategy:

Scripture Reference: _____

_____
_____
_____
_____
_____

Scripture Reference: _____

_____
_____
_____
_____
_____

List practical ways in which you can begin to implement each strategy into your stepparenting:

_____
_____
_____
_____
_____
_____
_____
_____
_____

Choose one item from your list which you will incorporate immediately. Pray and commit your plan to the Lord, ask Him for His direction and wisdom in implementation:

_____
_____
_____
_____
_____
_____
_____
_____
_____
_____

Without justice, *Compassion* is stripped of its *Wonder.*

STURDY LOVE

Dana held out hope they would recover from the latest financial crisis. They made more than enough money, but her husband continued to mismanage their income. Dana and Mike chatted with their pastor, a financial counselor, and a therapist. Mike had narrow ideas about gender roles in marriage. He would not release the handling of the household budget, although Dana possessed a global finance degree, and reported directly to the comptroller of the company where she worked. Dana was trying to be a "good wife" but found it difficult to submit to a man who did not know what he was doing. His mindless handling of the finances, and lust for material things, pushed them to the brink of bankruptcy. Dana was scared. She had never been in a financially precarious position before marrying Mike. She was also angry. After much prayer, she decided to take action. "Mike, I will not deposit my pay into the joint account anymore. You are not doing a good job with the finances and you will not accept any help from me, even though this is my area of expertise. I will handle the utilities. I will manage my own investments. I will make sure there is food in the house to eat. You will have to pay the mortgage and all of the consumer debt you created. You will not listen, and I will not allow you to continue to dig us into a hole without consequences." Mike was livid. His salary alone would not enable him to cover the mortgage, child support, all of his debts, and still have fun money. Admittedly, he became a bit more extravagant when he and Dana married, and she threw her six-figure salary into the pot. Dana, refused to cave in to Mike's tantrum. He was going to have to feel this.

Paul wrote in Romans:

Love must be sincere. Hate what is evil; cling to what is good.

Romans 12:9

Paul uses a strong word here. It is the Greek word, apostygountes. That word implies intense, violent hatred. God's love is patient, kind, thoughtful, humble, and everything else listed in 1 Corinthians 13, but don't let that lull you into a faulty belief that it pulls punches. Real love stands in direct opposition to sin. It sees sin for what it is; a threat to the freedom and wholeness of the person loved. So intense in its violent hatred for evil, sin, and disobedience that it steps in to rescue. Compassionately dedicated to the good of the loved one. This kind of love is sturdy, substantial, and true.

How did Dana demonstrate sturdy love?

_____
_____
_____
_____
_____

What might she do to help Mike realize she is acting in his best interest?

_____
_____
_____
_____
_____

Gut check. What do you "hate" about your own behavior in your stepfamily? For what do you need to repent?

_____
_____
_____
_____
_____

What is worthy of hate (truly sinful) in your bonus children's behavior? From what, in them, do they need to be rescued?

_____
_____
_____
_____

What is just annoying to you, vs sin trapping them?

_____
_____
_____
_____
_____

THIS AND THAT

And He passed in front of Moses, proclaiming, "The Lord, the Lord, the compassionate and gracious God, slow to anger, abounding in love and faithfulness, maintaining love to thousands, and forgiving wickedness, rebellion and sin. Yet he does not leave the guilty unpunished; he punishes the children and their children for the sin of the parents to the third and fourth generation."

Exodus 34:6-7

God's wrath and love complement each other. A Stepmom focused on loving while waiting to be loved dispenses a Holy Spirit led mixture of steady compassion and sturdy assessment.

What does this duality of God's nature mean to you personally?

_____
_____
_____
_____
_____

What does this mean for your stepparenting?

_____
_____
_____
_____
_____

I listed the actions that helped me grow in sturdy love. Put each into your own words:

1. Protect your peace.

   _____
   _____
   _____
   _____

2. Be honest about sin.

   _____
   _____
   _____
   _____

3. Realize that seasons come to an end.

   _____
   _____
   _____
   _____

4. Someone loves this child more than you do.

   _____
   _____
   _____
   _____

5. Don't stop praying

   _____
   _____
   _____
   _____

6. Carry your own luggage.

   _____
   _____
   _____
   _____

7. Trust God

   _____
   _____
   _____
   _____

8. Neutralize your interactions.

   _____
   _____
   _____
   _____

9. Celebrate what should be celebrated.

   _____
   _____
   _____
   _____

10. Let Wisdom Speak (James 3:13-18).

    _____
    _____
    _____
    _____

TREASURE HUNT

Read 2 Samuel, chapters 11 and 12.

Why did Nathan confront David?

_____
_____
_____
_____
_____

What techniques did Nathan use to confront David?

_____
_____
_____
_____
_____

Now read Ezekiel 34:23-25

What is the end of David's story?

_____
_____
_____
_____

In what ways does this strengthen the hope you have for your own children and family?

_____
_____
_____
_____
_____

Be a **brave** Stepmom:

the fruit is out on the *limb.*

WRITE YOUR STEPMOM MISSION STATEMENT

When I started my stepmom journey, I was very focused on "getting it right", being a blessing, and minimizing mistakes. However, I often found myself off track as I surrendered to feelings of inadequacy, resentment, and more. In those moments, knowing my "why" wasn't enough. I needed a concrete, easy to recall reminder to help me recalibrate. I prayed and developed a Stepmom Mission Statement.

A mission statement is a one or two sentence summary of your goals which include your call to live out your message, through a task, for a specific impact on the people you're called to reach.

Here's mine:

I influence my children to know and love God by encouraging them in His plans for their lives, demonstrating His love, and parenting for His glory, not my own.

My personal mission statement for the stepmoms I get to serve is:

I use the platform God gave me to: care for, equip, empower, and encourage stepmoms to thrive in their God-given role to love children not biologically their own, and receive their "Well Done."

Each statement reveals my message, my task, my impact, and my people. It reminds me that God has invited us to partner with Him in His work in the lives of those around us.

It can be challenging to create a mission statement. Carve out time for prayer and self-reflection. You also need a good set of questions to get your juices flowing. This exercise is designed to stimulate your mind, engage your heart, and help you form a concise mission statement for your role. Remember, you have been created anew in Christ Jesus to accomplish the good works God laid up for you in eternity past. (Ephesians 2:10). God foresaw you in this role and He attached Kingdom purpose to your presence in the lives of your husband and children. Sis, there is good work for you to accomplish in your family.

Ask the Holy Spirit to help you as you navigate through these. Grab a pen, your bible, and a cup of tea. Shut the door, turn off the phone, and let's get to work.

CREATING YOUR STEPMOM MISSION STATEMENT

1. Define your message (What are you trying to say?)

What are you always talking passionately about? What themes do you come back to when you are serving others?

_____
_____
_____
_____
_____

What have you been through that you can speak to? Ex: My stepmom friend witnessed physical abuse in her family of origin. She used her experiences to help her stepdaughter heal from trauma.

_____
_____
_____
_____
_____

What are people looking for when they come to you? What questions do you answer for them?

_____
_____
_____
_____
_____

In what areas do you have an unusual impact? Ex: I have a friend who draws women who have been hurt by relationship issues. God has anointed her to connect with and minister to them in ways which bring restoration and hope.

_____
_____
_____
_____
_____

Where is Jesus apparent in your life? Where has His transforming power worked in your life?

_____
_____
_____
_____
_____

People notice your life messages. Ask others to provide input or confirm your insights.

_____
_____
_____
_____
_____

2. **To whom are you speaking? (Who is your audience?)**

This is a relatively easy question to answer, however, your mission should be tailor-made to your audience. See mine for examples.

_____
_____
_____

3. **Impact (What are you going to accomplish?)**

    What do you want to see as a result of your influence on your children?

    _____
    _____
    _____
    _____
    _____

    How do you want to change their outward circumstances?

    _____
    _____
    _____
    _____
    _____

    How will your message touch their hearts?

    _____
    _____
    _____
    _____
    _____

    What blessing will you bring to them?

    _____
    _____
    _____
    _____
    _____

4. When they eulogize you, what do you want them to remember about you?

_____
_____
_____
_____
_____

5. Task (How are you going to do it?)

What tasks are you drawn to that might be great conduits for your message? Ex. I regularly spent time with each child, separately, doing what they loved. This allowed me to demonstrate His unique love for each of them and build relationship equity so I could influence them.

_____
_____
_____
_____
_____

What have you done in the past which conveys your message? What tasks would let you do more of that?

_____
_____
_____
_____
_____

How does your child speak love? Acts of kindness? Quality time? Words of Affirmation? Physical touch? Acts of service? Learn how to communicate love in the way they can understand it?

_____
_____
_____
_____
_____

Now, take all of your notes and distill them down to a simple and memorable one or two sentence statement. Play around with it until you come up with something you like.

_____
_____
_____
_____
_____
_____
_____
_____
_____
_____
_____
_____
_____
_____

SCRIPTURE MEDITATION

Turn to the Plant Your Heart chapter in your book. Use the lines below to record, and answer questions for, three of the scriptures on which the Holy Spirit focuses your attention.

Scripture reference: _____
Written Scripture
_____
_____
_____
_____
_____

How is the Holy Spirit encouraging me through this scripture?

_____
_____
_____
_____
_____

How is the Holy Spirit challenging me through this scripture?

_____
_____
_____
_____
_____

Scripture reference: _____
Written Scripture

_____
_____
_____
_____
_____

How is the Holy Spirit encouraging me through this scripture?

_____
_____
_____
_____
_____

How is the Holy Spirit challenging me through this scripture?

_____
_____
_____
_____
_____

Scripture reference: _____
Written Scripture

_____
_____
_____
_____
_____

How is the Holy Spirit encouraging me through this scripture?

_____
_____
_____
_____
_____

How is the Holy Spirit challenging me through this scripture?

_____
_____
_____
_____
_____

What other observations have I made?

_____
_____
_____
_____
_____

SECTION II NOTES

Abandon yourself to the *Kingdom* agenda attached to your step-parenting.

SECTION III

The Fruitful Heart

Praise God, Who has enabled me to love!

"You who seek God, may your hearts live!"

Psalm 69:32b

MARVELING MOMS

I shared my rainbow story to remind you that God is present and active in your life. But nothing is more powerful than your own story. Write your rainbow story: a time when you knew God was with you in your present circumstances.

_____
_____
_____
_____
_____
_____
_____
_____
_____
_____
_____
_____
_____
_____
_____

Which of God's attributes cause your heart to marvel?

_____
_____
_____
_____
_____

What stepmom moment has made you pause in praise unto God?

_____
_____
_____
_____
_____

You did not choose me, but I chose you and appointed you so that you might go and bear fruit—fruit that will last—and so that whatever you ask in my name the Father will give you.

John 15:16

Jesus calls us, "Chosen." Look at the list from Romans 8. Which of our "new life" realities bring you the most joy?

_____
_____
_____
_____
_____
_____
_____
_____
_____
_____

What was

insurmountable

is now

conquerable.

FIRST AND FOREMOST

Take a moment to read the parable of the Lost Son:

Jesus continued: There was a man who had two sons. The younger one said to his father, 'Father, give me my share of the estate.' So he divided his property between them.

Not long after that, the younger son got together all he had, set off for a distant country and there squandered his wealth in wild living. After he had spent everything, there was a severe famine in that whole country, and he began to be in need. So he went and hired himself out to a citizen of that country, who sent him to his fields to feed pigs. He longed to fill his stomach with the pods that the pigs were eating, but no one gave him anything.

When he came to his senses, he said, 'How many of my father's hired servants have food to spare, and here I am starving to death! I will set out and go back to my father and say to him: Father, I have sinned against heaven and against you. I am no longer worthy to be called your son; make me like one of your hired servants.' So he got up and went to his father.

But while he was still a long way off, his father saw him and was filled with compassion for him; he ran to his son, threw his arms around him and kissed him. The son said to him, 'Father, I have sinned against heaven and against you. I am no longer worthy to be called your son.'

But the father said to his servants, 'Quick! Bring the best robe and put it on him. Put a ring on his finger and sandals on his feet. Bring the fattened calf and kill it. Let's have a feast and celebrate. For this son of mine was dead and is alive again; he was lost and is found.' So they began to celebrate.

Meanwhile, the older son was in the field. When he came near the house, he heard music and dancing. So he called one of the servants and asked him what was going on. 'Your brother has come,' he replied, 'and your father has killed the fattened calf because he has him back safe and sound.'

The older brother became angry and refused to go in. So his father went out and pleaded with him. But he answered his father, 'Look! All these years I've been slaving for you and never disobeyed your orders. Yet you never gave me even a young goat so I could celebrate with my friends. But when this son of yours who has squandered your property with prostitutes comes home, you kill the fattened calf for him!'

'My son,' the father said, 'you are always with me, and everything I have is yours. But we had to celebrate and be glad, because this brother of yours was dead and is alive again; he was lost and is found.'

Luke 15:11-32

What goes on in your heart you when you sense the distance of a child living in or visiting your home?

_____
_____
_____
_____
_____

What do you think is "good" to do while you wait on this child to turn towards you?

_____
_____
_____
_____
_____

ALLIED BONUS MOM

Paul wrote to the saints in Thessalonica:

Just as a nursing mother cares for her children, so we cared for you. Because we loved you so much, we were delighted to share with you not only the gospel of God but our lives as well.

1 Thessalonians 2:7b-8

Paul "mothered" without being a mother. In what ways can you share your life, and the gospel, with your bonus children?

_____
_____
_____
_____
_____

Love is never competitive. Nor does it provoke jealousy. You are not responsible for someone else's perspective, but you are responsible for your intent. How might you love like a mother without deliberately provoking bio-mom to jealousy or insecurity? (Think along the lines of inclusiveness, warmth, etc.)

_____
_____
_____
_____
_____

How can you be a better ally to bio-mom? Again, you are only responsible for your own intent and actions.

_____
_____
_____
_____
_____

Why would it be important to respect the boundaries of bio-mom, whether living or dead, while still sharing your life with your bonus children?

_____
_____
_____
_____
_____

FROM HEAD TO HEART

Moving from head to heart is a journey that involves a deep look at motivation. According to Proverbs 4:23, everything begins in the heart; the ruling center of a person, our conscience, our mind, will, and emotion. From the heart springs our desires, our driving force, our manners, and beliefs. It is so vital to our overall wellbeing the bible warns us to guard our hearts more than anything else we guard. Over and over again, Jesus demonstrated He was far more concerned about the heart of a person than the habits of a person. In His sermon on the mount (Matthew 5-7), He repeats the phrase, "You have heard it said…" followed by a point of law. He then places an addendum on the law by saying, "But, I say…" followed by a challenge to the listener's motivation.

What are some of the "But I say" statements you are challenged with in your stepparenting? (Think about some the things you have been told or believe about being a stepmother or serving self that contradicts what the bible says about loving and serving others.):

_____
_____
_____
_____
_____

Jesus intends truth in our heads to liberate our hearts. In what ways can you give God both your head and your heart?

_____
_____
_____
_____
_____

Worry clogs the pathway between our heads and hearts. What one thing would you like to stop worrying about in your stepmothering?

_____
_____
_____

_____
_____
_____

Philippians 4:6-7 reads: *"Do not be anxious about anything, but in every situation, by prayer and petition, with thanksgiving, present your requests to God. And the peace of God, which transcends all understanding, will guard your hearts and your minds in Christ Jesus."* Take a moment to pray about the issue worrying you. Thank God for taking care of this need. Pray about it until you sense His peace silencing the thoughts in your mind and calming the turmoil in your heart.

SEE THE LORD

The clearer picture you have of who you are serving, the easier it is to stay focused on Him.

In the year that King Uzziah died, I saw the Lord, high and exalted, seated on a throne; and the train of his robe filled the temple. Above him were seraphim, each with six wings: With two wings they covered their faces, with two they covered their feet, and with two they were flying. And they were calling to one another:

"Holy, holy, holy is the Lord Almighty; the whole earth is full of his glory."
Isaiah 6:1-3

What feels imposing in your family life today?

_____
_____
_____
_____
_____

How does it compare to God?

_____
_____
_____

_____
_____

Read Psalm 18 and Psalm 145

Use these Psalms to describe God?

_____
_____
_____
_____
_____

Jesus is my Savior, Lord, King and Shepherd. He is also my Friend, my Healer, my Hero, and the Light of my life. Who do you say that He is?

_____
_____
_____
_____
_____

FILL UP AND TILT YOUR HEART

I pray that out of his glorious riches he may strengthen you with power through his Spirit in your inner being, so that Christ may dwell in your hearts through faith. And I pray that you, being rooted and established in love, may have power, together with all the Lord's holy people, to grasp how wide and long and high and deep is the love of Christ, and to know this love that surpasses knowledge—that you may be filled to the measure of all the fullness of God.

Ephesians 3:16-19

Being inspired by the Holy Spirit, Paul writes this prayer. How does knowing the prayer above is God's will for your life encourage you?

_____
_____

_____
_____
_____
_____

We grant God greater access to our hearts for infilling by tilting our hearts towards Him. Some approaches we listed in the book were:

Ask: Luke records Jesus' words in Luke 11:13 "If you then, though you are evil, know how to give good gifts to your children, how much more will your Father in heaven give the Holy Spirit to those who ask him!"

Obey: Obedience conforms our lives, thoughts, and ways to His life, thoughts and ways. Obedience aligns our hearts with His heart. Obedience brings us into intimate fellowship and friendship with Him.

Prayer: Prayer is the means by which we communicate with, acknowledge, and invite the activity of God into our daily life. Prayer focuses our hearts on hearing from a God who hears and answers. (Psalm 91:15, Isaiah 65:24)

Worship: Worship exalts God and acknowledges His worthiness. The Bible tells us God inhabits the praises of His people (Psalm 22:3). When we worship the Lord, He meets with us. We encounter His presence and experience the fullness of joy. (Psalm 16:11)

Communion: The act of remembering and celebrating Jesus' death on the cross for our sins (1 Peter 3:18) keeps us focused on the covenant lovingly ratified in the blood of Jesus.

Stillness: The Psalmist wrote: "My heart is not proud, Lord, my eyes are not haughty; I do not concern myself with great matters or things too wonderful for me. But I have calmed and quieted myself, I am like a weaned child with its mother; like a weaned child I am content." (Psalm 131:1-2) In stillness we come to know God in the way He wishes to reveal Himself and learn to be content with Him alone.

In what other ways can you tilt your heart towards the Lord? What provokes worship and notice in your heart? (i.e., I notice God's presence by the ocean.)

_____
_____
_____
_____
_____

WHEN LOST ONES COME HOME

The beauty of the father's response to his once lost son causes my heart to swell. There was no rebuke. No, "I told you so." No punishing demotion. Upon his return home, the young man was immediately restored to status. The father returned both the ring and the robe, signifying his reclamation of the son once lost to him. The father received him with love and hoopla.

What does the father's response tell you about God, the Father?

_____
_____
_____
_____
_____

What does the father's response tell you about how you should respond to the return of your lost ones?

_____
_____
_____
_____
_____

Jesus said in Luke 15:10:

"In the same way, I tell you, there is rejoicing in the presence of the angels of God over one sinner who repents."

Paint a picture of your "homecoming" celebration in heaven. Describe the colors and activities. Who cheered you on? Who for you rejoiced?

_____
_____
_____
_____
_____

TREASURE HUNT

Have you identified a "lost one" in your family? If so, who?

_____

How might God be growing you through your relationship with him/her?

_____
_____
_____
_____
_____

What disciplines is God asking you to incorporate in order to deepen the tilt of your heart towards Him?

_____
_____
_____
_____
_____

Write out a prayer for the lost one in your home:

_____
_____
_____
_____
_____

Ask the Lord to help you know Him better. Over the next few days, notice and record His answers to this prayer.

_____
_____
_____
_____
_____

No one is *unseen* by the Father!

MY FATHER'S EYES

My beloved hubby owns an IT Security corporation. His first degree was in accounting. His second is in information technology. He is decidedly left-brained. I, on the other hand, am an author, bible teacher, and speaker, with a mild case of ADHD, and a penchant for adventure. We definitely approach life from different points of view. We work so well together though, it's more comical than frustrating. Our differences were vividly on display during a trip to South Africa. My thoughts were along the lines of, "This is a once in a lifetime trip. I am going to wring every day dry of adventure." Jonathan was more measured. For instance, on safari one morning, we came across a cheetah lounging in the sun. My instinctive response was to lie down in the brush about 15 feet away, well within the one leap distance, and take pictures. I was having the time of my life. Jonathan thought I had lost my mind. I saw an exciting opportunity to live out my wildlife photographer fantasy in a relatively safe environment. Jonathan started formulating his "reasons why Cheryl did not come home from Africa alive" speech. I, however, got the "money shot!"

Perspective is the way we see something; the interpretation of information in relationship to ourselves. It is shaped by the experiences, values, states of mind, belief systems, and assumptions which we bring into each and every situation.

LOOK AGAIN

Let's read Acts 15:36-41:

Sometime later Paul said to Barnabas, "Let us go back and visit the believers in all the towns where we preached the word of the Lord and see how they are doing." Barnabas wanted to take John, also called Mark, with them, but Paul did not think it wise to take him, because he had deserted them in Pamphylia and had not continued with them in the work. They had such a sharp disagreement that they parted company. Barnabas took Mark and sailed for Cyprus, but Paul chose Silas and left, commended by the believers to the grace of the Lord. He went through Syria and Cilicia, strengthening the churches.

Paul's experience with Mark, left a sour taste in his mouth. He felt so strongly about Mark, he split from his mentor, Barnabas.

Find a quiet space and take your time with this question. What does your experience with your stepchildren tell you about them?

_____
_____
_____
_____
_____

How may your perspective be skewed?

_____
_____
_____
_____
_____

One Saturday in a park, the Lord arrested my attention to deposit truth in my heart. His words to me were, "You will never look into the eyes of someone whom I do not love nor for whom Christ did not die!" What does this tell you about your relationship with your bonus children?

_____
_____
_____
_____
_____

If you and I can look at our bonus children through the eyes of the Father, and value them based on His perspective, rather than their actions, we will obtain access to their hearts.

What obstacles to changing your perspective have you run into in this area of your relationship with your bonus children? What has made it hard for you to see them through the eyes of Jesus?

_____

_____
_____
_____
_____
_____

How do you think God might want to meet you in this area?

_____
_____
_____
_____
_____

BY CHRIST, BEHELD

The bible tells us that the very hairs on our heads are numbered (Luke 12:7). Jesus has you completely memorized. The shape of every freckle, wrinkle, healed scar, and birthmark is known by Him. He knows that, instead of scratching, you twitch your nose when it's tickled. He knows that you love the smell of cinnamon and feel deliciously small at the ocean. His unreserved contemplation goes beyond physical attributes and quirky behavior. He is intimately acquainted with your secret thoughts, desires, and intimidations. He is a beholder of you.

How does this reality comfort you? Unnerve you?

_____
_____
_____
_____
_____

Why?

_____
_____
_____
_____
_____

The intimate inspection of Jesus communicates His great love. To be known and wanted is the urgent plea of mankind. Jesus answers this cry in every way. He often uses others to communicate His love for and interest in us.

What emotions bubble up knowing He wants to use your eyes to behold your bonus children and communicate His love?

_____
_____
_____
_____
_____

THE UNFAIRNESS OF IT ALL

Julia and Nate began to treat Liam as they saw him, not as his actions warranted. Without curbing consequences, they remained gracious and compassionate towards him.

In what ways do you find their approach challenging? Inspiring?

_____
_____
_____
_____
_____

God is absolutely not fair. He is good to people who hate Him. He allows bad things to happen to people who love Him. Want and disease occur in the lives of people who praise Him. Healing and prosperity occur in the lives of people who do not acknowledge Him.

Jeremiah wrote in Lamentations:

"Yet this I call to mind and therefore I have hope: Because of the Lord's great love we are not consumed, for His compassion never fails. They are new every morning; great is your faithfulness."

(v. 21-23)

And Ezra wrote in his namesake book:

"What has happened to us is a result of our evil deeds and our great guilt, and yet, our God, you have punished us less than our sins deserved and have given us a remnant like this."

(Ezra 9:13)

In what ways, if any, does your approach to parenting need to change to incorporate more mercy than punishment or more accountability than mercy? (Consider attitudes, actions like stonewalling, silence, and passive-aggressive responses)

_____
_____
_____
_____
_____

MUST HAVES

We may tussle with our emotions, our family structures, the fatigue of blended family living, but our family dynamics are exactly what we need to keep us dependent on the Lord. God employs the complications for our good.

Using the list in the book (refine us, humble us, focus us, etc.), how is God using the challenges of your family?

_____

What do you think is meant by "what was has to die in order to make room for the beauty we enjoy"?

What imperfections in your family (stepchildren, husband, children, yourself) has been a disappointment to you?

What changes can "eyes full of faith" bring to how you view your family?

TREASURE HUNT

Take an "inventory" of your bonus children. What glimpses of God's fingerprint do you see in their lives?

- ◊ Natural gifts and talents
- ◊ Activities which bring them joy
- ◊ Ways in which they show love, and kindness

Child **Inventory**

_____ _____
_____
_____
_____
_____

_____ _____
_____
_____
_____
_____

_____ _____
_____
_____
_____
_____

_____ _____
_____
_____
_____
_____

How might you encourage their gifts or show an interest in their interests? (Sign up for a class with them. Learn about the activity. Surprise them with homemade chemistry experiments if they're good at science. Get creative.)

_____
_____
_____
_____
_____
_____

What issues or challenges are dampening the impact of those things you inventoried?

_____
_____
_____
_____
_____
_____

Pray for them. Ask the Lord to help you see them as He does. Ask Him to keep you aware of opportunities for encouragement and planting seeds. Ask Him to teach you how to speak life over them. Ask the Lord to strengthen them to overcome their challenges, and to heal them from emotional pain.

_____
_____
_____
_____
_____
_____

Jesus

has pledged

Himself

to you and me

SAFE SHEPHERDS

Steffanie recalled how much she loved her second stepmom. Her father had "gifted" her life with three. Steffanie's first stepmother was the result of an affair she had with Steffanie's father. The last one, a greedy woman 25 years her father's junior, outlived Steffanie's dad. Her second stepmom was a gem. She was loving and welcoming. Steffanie never refers to any other of her father's wives as her stepmom. Only Susan holds that honor. Even after her father unceremoniously dumped Susan for a younger model, Steffanie remained close to her. Susan married Steffanie's father when Steffanie was an awkward 13-year-old. For seven years Steffanie had a confidant, and a champion, who insisted Steffanie's dad did more than spend money on Steffanie. Susan was Steffanie's safe place and remained so long after she was no longer officially Steffanie's stepmom. Steffanie's children called her, "Bubbie." Because of Susan's loving concern, and prayers, Steffanie was able to forgive her father, and become a follower of Christ.

God is our refuge, sanctuary, and hiding place. We can trust Him with our most authentic selves. He sees it all and welcomes us still. He lovingly shows us Mommas how to hold sacred space in which our children experience His grace and mercy. He teaches us to shepherd: to lead, guide, love, and minister. He teaches us to shelter: to create a refuge where they are at ease, transparent, and accepted.

Jesus' shepherding provides:

Intimacy & Belonging *John 10:14-15*	Provision *Psalm 23:2*
Protection *Psalm 23:4*	Respite and Rest *Revelations 7:17*
Specificity *John 10:16*	Safety and Shelter *John 10:28-29*
Healing *Psalm 23:5*	Sacrificial Love *John 10:11*
Recovery *Luke 15:4*	Reward *1 Peter 5:4*

As recipients of our Shepherd's care, you and I are called to shepherd in our family.

Considering what Jesus provides, what does it mean to you to be a shepherd in your home?

_____
_____
_____
_____
_____

What does it mean to you to be a safe place?

_____
_____
_____
_____
_____

In what ways do you feel adequate or inadequate to provide that type of care?

_____
_____
_____
_____
_____

Peter wrote in his first letter:

> *To the elders among you, I appeal as a fellow elder and a witness of Christ's sufferings who also will share in the glory to be revealed: Be shepherds of God's flock that is under your care, watching over them—not because you must, but because you are willing, as God wants you to be; not pursuing dishonest gain, but eager to serve; not lording it over those entrusted to you, but being examples to the flock. And when the Chief Shepherd appears, you will receive the crown of glory that will never fade away.*
> 1 Peter 5:1-4

Friend, you may not be an elder in a church body, but you are an elder in your home. As a mom in your home, you are part of the Chief Shepherd's team. You have been called to your family to lead, guide, care for, and protect the children entrusted to you by God. For however long, and at whatever interval, they are in your care.

Which item(s) on the list of "safe mom" characteristics is/are embedded in your stepmomming? How do you know?

_____
_____
_____
_____
_____

Where do you need growth?

_____
_____
_____
_____
_____

SHEPHERED TOO

The safe place built for others is sacred space set aside for those you shepherd and for you. A space made where you can be yourself, connect on a deep level, and hear the truth about your own flaws without defensiveness because you know what is shared is encased in love. Safety given. Safety returned.

In what ways, if any, have you been shepherded by the people in your family?

_____
_____
_____
_____
_____

What did you experience as a result of being shepherded?

_____
_____
_____
_____
_____

TREASURE HUNT

Read Psalm 23 and the 10th Chapter of John.

What characteristics of our Good Shepherd speak to you?

_____
_____
_____
_____
_____

How has God shown Himself to be a shepherd in your life?

_____
_____
_____
_____
_____

In what ways is the Lord challenging you to shepherd your family?

_____
_____
_____
_____
_____

Ask the Holy Spirit to show you the importance of your ministry to your stepchildren.

Nothing lays beyond Jesus' ability to *change*

THIS HEART IS ON FIRE

One of the best things we can do for our families is have a passionate pursuit of God.

Paul wrote to the Philippians:

But whatever were gains to me I now consider loss for the sake of Christ. What is more, I consider everything a loss because of the surpassing worth of knowing Christ Jesus my Lord, for whose sake I have lost all things. I consider them garbage, that I may gain Christ and be found in him, not having a righteousness of my own that comes from the law, but that which is through faith in Christ the righteousness that comes from God on the basis of faith. I want to know Christ yes, to know the power of his resurrection and participation in his sufferings, becoming like him in his death, and so, somehow, attaining to the resurrection from the dead.

Philippians 3:7-11

Describe your relationship with God? What does it look like?

_____
_____
_____
_____
_____

What good things in your life are competing with Jesus for preeminence in your affections?

_____
_____
_____
_____
_____

What do those things give you that keep you coming back to them rather than God?

_____
_____
_____
_____
_____

What percentage of time do you feel you are in alignment with your primary calling to worship and glorify God?

_____
_____
_____
_____
_____

What changes do you need to make to increase that percentage?

_____
_____
_____
_____
_____

KNOWING GOD

Many of us would say knowing God is high on our priority list. However, to know God, is to experience Him. That means in order to know Jehovah Rapha, the God who heals, you must first be sick. In order to know God as provider, you must first experience lack. I did not know God as defender until I was in what I thought was an indefensible position. We often forfeit the joy of intimacy with God by shrinking back from the difficulties of life.

In what ways has God revealed Himself through your circumstances?

_____
_____
_____

_____
_____

What did you learn about God?

_____
_____
_____
_____
_____

What ignited in your heart as a result of becoming newly acquainted with an aspect of God's nature?

_____
_____
_____
_____
_____

THE MINISTRY OF STEPMOMMING

You and I have been perfectly positioned to make a God-sized difference in the lives of our stepchildren. For us, being a stepmother is more than being the wife of some child's father. We are ambassadors of Christ, called to preach the gospel in word and deed to our bonus children.

What is the impact of your ministry to your bonus children? Is it evident?

_____
_____
_____
_____
_____

How do you evaluate the effectiveness of your ministry to your bonus children?

_____
_____
_____
_____
_____

What has been holding you back from effective ministry to your bonus children?

_____
_____
_____
_____
_____

It is more important that your stepchildren receive the gospel than it is they receive it from you. If your bonus children are not receptive to you, ask the Lord to soften their hearts and lead them to the person from whom they can receive the gospel?

_____
_____
_____
_____
_____

THE WORSHIP OF STEPMOMMMING

The entire purpose of our lives is to bring praise and honor to God. Any role we assume in life is executed as an outward expression of reverence for the One to whom belongs all the glory. Stepmomming is our worship.

Describe worship and its impact on your stepmothering?

_____
_____
_____
_____
_____

Godly worship is comprehensive in its scope, covering all of life. What applications can you make to incorporate a greater sense of worship in the mundane tasks of life?

_____
_____
_____
_____
_____

What are some practical ways in which you can demonstrate worship in your stepmothering?

_____
_____
_____
_____
_____

Distractions abound. To keep the fire of worship burning, we have to stoke the flame. How will you keep your heart stoked and the distractions doused?

_____
_____
_____
_____
_____

THE WITNESS OF STEPMOMMING

In what ways are your stepchildren drawn to Christ through you?

_____
_____
_____
_____
_____

Have you ever shared your salvation story with your bonus children? What was their response? If you haven't, use the space to write out your story to be shared.

_____
_____
_____
_____
_____

If Jesus were to take an inventory of your attitude towards your bonus children, what of Himself would He see reflected there?

_____
_____
_____
_____
_____

To imitate Christ in our step-mothering is to give ourselves up to loving. Totally. Go all in. Walk in the way of love without reservation. What restraint do you need to remove from your love for your bonus children?

_____
_____
_____
_____
_____

TREASURE HUNT

How has your family benefited from you knowing God?

_____
_____
_____
_____
_____

Read Ephesians 1:3-12

How does it make you feel to know you are already wanted?

_____
_____
_____
_____
_____

Write out a prayer of thanksgiving praising God for choosing you to be His hands and feet in your family and sealing you for His purposes.

_____
_____
_____
_____
_____
_____
_____
_____
_____
_____
_____
_____
_____
_____

THE DEVOTED LIFE

One of the best gifts we can give our families is our personal, passionate, pursuit of God. It is also one of the best gifts to give yourself. One year from now you could be walking more closely with God; in greater victory over sin, greater love for those around you, greater freedom from the dynamics which send you reeling today. It will happen one day, one prayer, and one choice at a time. You need only commit to the most important call in your life: devotion to God.

Scripture Memory Verse: One thing have I asked of the Lord, that will I seek after, that I may dwell in the house of the Lord all the days of my life, to gaze upon the beauty of the Lord and to seek Him in His temple. (Psalm 27:4)

What does a devoted life look like to you? Describe both the qualities and habits of a person who lives a devoted life:

_____
_____
_____
_____
_____

What changes do you need to make in your schedule or lifestyle to allow you to consistently spend time with the Lord?

_____
_____
_____
_____
_____

Remember, we are not exchanging "to don'ts" for "to dos". God wants relationship with us. Discipline helps us with consistency, but the goal is not another religious practice. The goal is to create opportunity and space for fellowship between you and your Heavenly Father.

Make the commitment. Nothing will happen until you decide. The privilege of knowing God is worth any adjustment or sacrifice you need to make. A devoted life will be specific to you but usually includes prayer, scripture meditation, worship, and journaling. If you are new to a devotional life, I strongly discourage you from incorporating all practices at the same time. Instead, choose one, make a plan, commit to it for 30 days, and record your observations.

At the end of the 30 days, you will have naturally created a habit designed to nurture an intimate relationship with the Lord.

30-Day Challenge Commitment:

I desire to grow in my walk with the Lord and to know Him more intimately. I commit to spend more time alone with the Lord.

For 30 days, beginning _____
                                              Insert Date

I will set aside _____ at _____
              Insert Amount of Time   *Insert Time of Day*

to _____
        Activity: Prayer, Reading of the Word, Worship, etc.

_____   _____
        Signature   *Today's Date*

SCRIPTURE MEDITATION

Turn to the Pour Your Heart chapter in your book. Use the lines below to record, and answer questions for, three of the scriptures on which the Holy Spirit focuses your attention.

Scripture reference: _____
Written Scripture
_____
_____
_____
_____
_____

How is the Holy Spirit encouraging me through this scripture?

_____
_____
_____
_____
_____

How is the Holy Spirit challenging me through this scripture?

_____
_____
_____
_____
_____
_____

Scripture reference: _____
Written Scripture

_____
_____
_____
_____
_____

How is the Holy Spirit encouraging me through this scripture?

_____
_____
_____
_____
_____

How is the Holy Spirit challenging me through this scripture?

_____
_____
_____
_____
_____

Scripture reference: _____
Written Scripture

_____
_____
_____
_____
_____

How is the Holy Spirit encouraging me through this scripture?
_____
_____
_____
_____
_____
_____

How is the Holy Spirit challenging me through this scripture?
_____
_____
_____
_____
_____
_____
_____

What other observations have I made?
_____
_____
_____
_____
_____
_____

SECTION III NOTES

The *Wait* is over: YOU ARE *Wanted!*

THE WAIT IS OVER

Although they are a more ingrained part of our culture, affirmations have been around for a long time. You have probably used them without realizing it. Have you ever stopped in the middle of a difficult task to pump yourself up with, "You got this"? That's an affirmation. It's a statement which shifts your focus away from perceived inadequacies and towards your strength and value.

There's a lot of brain science going on to move you from repetition to belief. That movement is harder when your affirmations are not based in reality or truth. So, although I believe affirmations can help change your mindset, I also believe they must be aligned in truth; as in, the Word of God.

Rather than random positive thoughts to repeat, let's speak truth. Because, the truth is you are already wanted. The truth is you are beloved. The truth is your future is greater than your past. The truth is no one compares to you. The truth is your mistakes do not disqualify you from God's plans for your life. The truth is God is for you!

I'm asking you to make it a practice to rehearse words based on the Word. Speak life over your heart. Write down 30 affirming truths, based on scripture, to remind yourself, as often as needed, what God has to say about you. I've helped you out by jotting down twenty. Search the scriptures for ten more.

30 AFFIRMING TRUTHS FOR STEPMOM

- ◊ I'm perfected, not perfect.
- ◊ I'm where God wants me to be.
- ◊ God has made me brave.
- ◊ God's power works best in my weakness
- ◊ God meets all of my needs
- ◊ I am a daughter of the King
- ◊ I am worth far more than rubies.
- ◊ I light up the world.
- ◊ God has good for me.
- ◊ I'm crowned with joy.

- ◊ Goodness and Mercy follow me.
- ◊ God has set my heart free.
- ◊ I am enabled by God's grace.
- ◊ I am rescued, redeemed, and restored.
- ◊ God fights for me.
- ◊ I am chosen to be loved.
- ◊ I wear dignity and strength.
- ◊ I am God's masterpiece.
- ◊ I live in peace.
- ◊ I overcome what I face.

- ◊ _____
- ◊ _____
- ◊ _____
- ◊ _____
- ◊ _____

- ◊ _____
- ◊ _____
- ◊ _____
- ◊ _____
- ◊ _____

LETTER FROM A BIO MOM

Dear Stepmom:

This is probably the hardest letter I have ever written, but I felt the need to let you know a few things. Your marriage to my kids' father was very difficult for me...at first. Not that I wanted him back, although I do admit I did not like watching him be a better husband to you than he was to me. I was more concerned with how you would get along with my children. Would you like them? Would you treat them well? Would their dad choose you and your children over his own? I was most worried about them liking you more than they do me. It sounds so silly now, but there it is.

See, I am their mother. I gave birth to them. I raised them. I love them. They love me too. Then again, so did their father. When you've been divorced, it's easy to believe anyone's love can be snatched away from you. You scared me. I felt threatened when you came along. I resented you. I just knew you were going to try to take my place. Remember when the waitress thought you were the kid's mom and I was the stepmom? That really ticked me off. But then, you know that. Everyone in the restaurant that night knows it! (LOL) That we can laugh about these things now says it all. I suppose I should confess I used to pump the kids for information about you. Petty, isn't it? You will be happy to know they never had anything bad to say about you.

Then, something happened. My mother died and you were there...for me. Not just for the kids, but me. You told me that we were family and that we would always be family. After we buried my mother, I started thinking about all of the times we interacted. Recently, someone I know said they thought you were a wonderful person. They didn't know we knew each other. I felt proud saying you were my kids' stepmom.

I want to apologize for the times I made things harder than they had to be. I want to thank you for your patience. I also want to thank you for loving our kids. It was a long time getting here, and took a longer time to admit, but I want you to know I appreciate you. If the kids had to have a bonus mom, I'm glad it's you.

God bless you,

Bio-Mom

Friend, you may never receive a letter like the one above. You may never receive verbal thanks, or even a smile. However, one day, you will hear, "Well done, good and faithful servant. Enter into the joy of the Lord!"

Keep Stepmomming in Grace,

Cheryl

RECCOMMENDED RESOURCES

BOOKS

- Nonviolent Communication (A Language of Life) by Marshall B. Rosenberg, PhD
- The Power of Knowing God by Dr. Tony Evans
- Spiritual Disciplines Handbook: Practices that Transform Us by Adele Ahlberg Calhoun
- The Smart Stepmom: Practical Steps to Help You Thrive by Ron L. Deal and Laura Petheridge
- Blended: Aligning the Hierarchy of Heart and Home by Summer Butler
- The Crucified Life: How to Live Out A Deeper Christian Experience by A.W. Tozer
- Love Like That: 5 Relationship Secrets from Jesus by Dr. Les Parrott
- Stepparenting with Grace: A Devotional for Blended Families by Gayla Grace
- Building Love Together in Blended Families: The 5 Love Languages and Becoming Stepfamily Smart by Gary Chapman, PhD and Ron L. Deal
- Desiring God, Revised Edition: Meditations of a Christian Hedonist by John Piper

WEBSITES

www.stepmomsanity.com
www.familylifeblended.com
www.blackandmarriedwithkids.com
www.focusonthefamily.com
www.stepparentingwithgrace.com
www.blendedkingdomfamilies.com
www.stepmommag.com

PODCASTS

Stepmom Sanity
Family Life Blended
The Nacho Kids Podcast
The Stepmom Club
The Stepmom Show

ACKNOWLEDGEMENTS

I am so grateful for the prayers, support, and handholding which helped me complete this workbook.

Thank you to the brilliant team at The Inspired Studio, LLC: Nicole Peavy (branding & design), Jamie Bonds, Luverta Reames (editor), and Serena Boyd and the ladies who, along with them, comprise the Stepmom Sanity team: Mom, Dr. Tahira Smith, and Germaine Simms. Thank you for praying, feedback, and keeping us on track.

To the Launch Team, thank you for being the first readers, reviewers, and trumpeters of Waiting to be Wanted. You are appreciated more than you know.

To the Tribe, my God-given sisters, thank you for being my safe place.

To my family, my supportive, loving, hero, Jonathan, thank you for your patience when my head was buried in my laptop for hours, hand rubs when my fingers were cold, and encouragement every time I doubted. To my children: my beautiful Peanut, Kayla, my bonus blessings, Chakia, Briana, and Jay; I am so grateful to the Lord for each you. You have filled my life with immeasurable joy.

Most important, to my Lord and Savior, Jesus Christ, to You be all the glory!

Hope for Stepmoms Who are There, From Stepmoms Who've Been There!

@StepmomSanity

www.StepmomSanity.com

www.ingramcontent.com/pod-product-compliance
Lightning Source LLC
Chambersburg PA
CBHW081507080526
44589CB00017B/2674